ARTIFICIAL INTELLIGENCE
and Other Computer Tech

World Book, Inc.
180 North LaSalle Street
Suite 900
Chicago, Illinois 60601
USA

For information about other "Cool Tech" titles, as well as other World Book print and digital publications, please go to www.worldbook.com.

For information about other World Book publications, call 1-800-WORLDBK (967-5325).

For information about sales to schools and libraries, call 1-800-975-3250 (United States) or 1-800-837-5365 (Canada).

Library of Congress Cataloging-in-Publication Data for this volume has been applied for.

Cool Tech
ISBN: 978-0-7166-2429-5 (set, hc.)

Artificial Intelligence and Other Computer Tech
ISBN: 978-0-7166-2437-0 (hc.)

Also available as:
ISBN: 978-0-7166-2454-7 (e-book)

2nd printing November 2021

STAFF

Editorial

Writer
Echo Elise González

Manager, New Content
Jeff De La Rosa

Manager, New Product Development
Nick Kilzer

Proofreader
Nathalie Strassheim

Manager, Contracts and Compliance (Rights and Permissions)
Loranne K. Shields

Manager, Indexing Services
David Pofelski

Digital

Director, Digital Product Development
Erika Meller

Digital Product Manager
Jonathan Wills

Graphics and Design

Senior Designer
Don DiSante

Media Editor
Rosalia Bledsoe

Manufacturing/ Production

Manufacturing Manager
Anne Fritzinger

Production Specialist
Curley Hunter

Credit: © Mike Dotta, Shutterstock

CONTENTS

Introduction 5

1 Artificial Intelligence 6

2 The Internet of Things 14

3 Smartphones 20

4 Brain-Computer Interface 24

5 Quantum Computers 30

6 Cryptocurrency 36

7 Internet 42

Glossary 46

Index 47

Acknowledgments 48

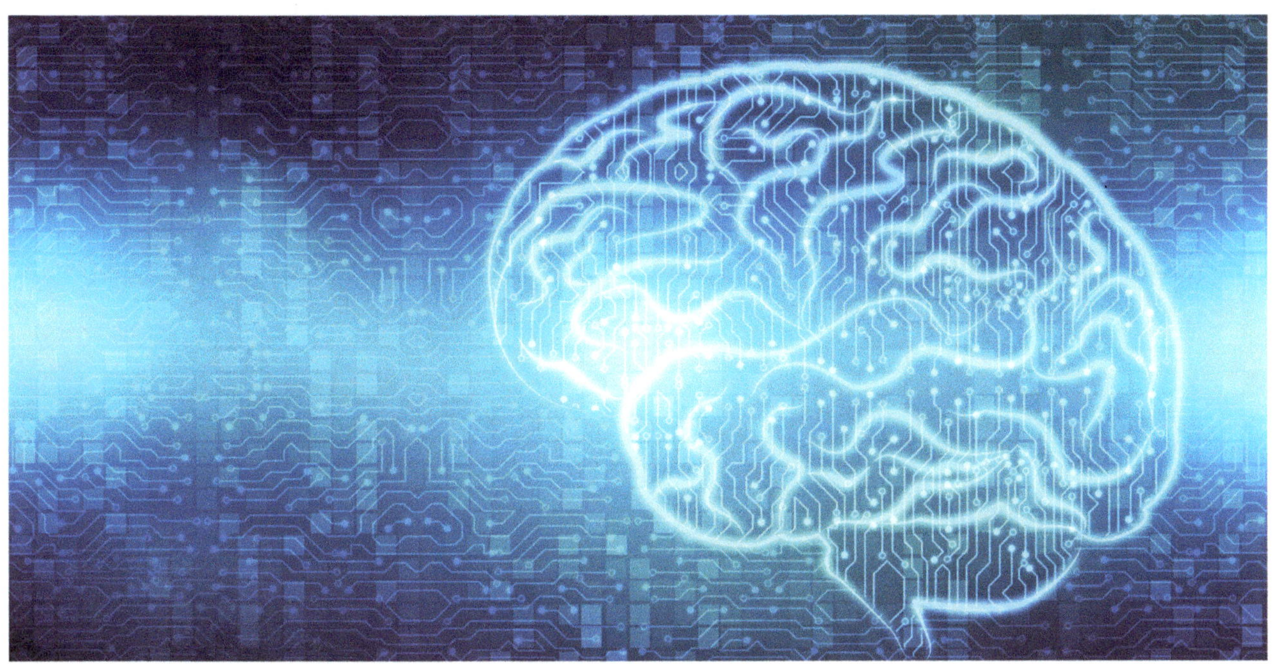

INTRODUCTION

Computers are everywhere. They're in phones, cars, elevators, video games, toasters, and even outer space. We use computers to perform a huge variety of tasks, from searching the internet to exploring the ocean, to flying airplanes. They even help us milk cows.

With computers affecting so many parts of our lives, it's exciting to think about how they will get more advanced in the coming years. Researchers are working to develop artificial intelligence that can allow a computer to think and learn in ways similar to human beings. Others are developing brain-computer **interface** technology that allows the user to control a computer with their mind. Meanwhile, computer scientists are working hard to create a true quantum computer—a special and unique kind of computer that is extremely fast and powerful.

Imagine how such advanced computers might change our lives in ten or twenty years, when computers will be even more ever-present in our world. Will we be able to use mind control to fly **drones?** Could we find a missing sock using a search engine? Will there be quantum robot maids that can clean our rooms in a matter of seconds? No one knows yet if these things will ever come to be, but this book explores the possibilities of a future with advanced computing.

1 ARTIFICIAL INTELLIGENCE

A SMART WORLD

Imagine waking up in the morning to the sound of your favorite song. You tell your alarm clock to turn off the song and turn on the lights. You ask your shower to turn on and warm up to 105 °F (41 °C). As you are drying your hair, you receive a text from your toaster that your bread has been toasted exactly as much as you like. You munch on the toast and ask your voice assistant what the weather is like today. Crumbs fall onto the floor, but not to worry because your smart vacuum will soon clean them up. The voice assistant tells you it's chilly outside, so you put on your smart jacket, which instantly heats up to your preferred body temperature. You head outside where a car is waiting to pick you up and take you to school. But there is no one else in the car because artificial intelligence (AI) will navigate the road this morning. In the self-driving car, you receive a text from your bot companion asking how you're feeling today. You chat for a while, and your artificial friend shares a funny memory, making you laugh.

This might sound like a futuristic scenario, but in fact all of these technologies are available today, thanks to AI. AI is the ability of a computer or other device to think, behave, or learn in a manner similar to humans. As the technology advances, AI is moving beyond the world of science fiction and into our real lives. AI can now be found inside the home, out on the streets, in our devices and vehicles, and even in outer space.

AI in outer space. CIMON is an AI robot that was created to keep astronauts company in outer space. CIMON stands for *Crew Interactive Mobile companiON*. It is a floating robot head that can play music, help astronauts with tasks, and more. It can even recognize the faces of its astronaut friends. CIMON is the first ever AI astronaut assistant.

GAME MASTERS

The idea of a machine beating a human being at any game, even tic-tac-toe, was once the stuff of dreams. Thanks to AI, today's computers are capable of beating humans at a range of complex games, from video games to chess. Mastering such complicated games requires a variety of *cognitive* (thinking) skills including strategizing, learning from experience, and anticipating the moves of the opponent. When a **computer program** masters a game, it is often seen as an important checkmark in AI development.

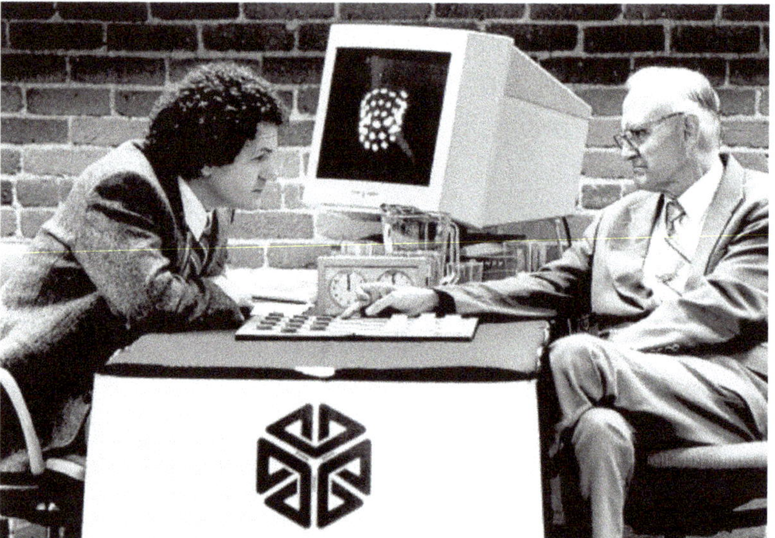

Checkers. In 1994, a computer program called Chinook won the World Checkers/Draughts Championship. This made Chinook the first computer program ever to win a world championship. The first AI to beat a human checkers master was a computer program created by AI researcher Arthur Samuel. The program's victory made people curious about AI. People began to imagine the possibilities of a future with *superintelligence* (intelligence far surpassing that of humans).

Chess. In 1996, Russian chess master Garry Kasparov defeated an IBM computer program called Deep Blue in a six-game chess competition. The following year, a more powerful Deep Blue defeated Kasparov in a rematch. Before Deep Blue's victory, many people believed that no computer program would ever be able to defeat a human at such a complex game.

Go. In 2015, Google's AlphaGo defeated the Chinese-born French Go champion Fan Hui. Go, a popular board game that has been played in Asia for thousands of years, is known for its complexity due to the high number of plays possible during each turn. AlphaGo used a kind of machine learning called deep learning to achieve victory. A deep learning computer program processes information through multiple layers of programmed *algorithms* (step-by-step procedures for solving problems). The program is able to learn complicated concepts by developing them from layers of simpler concepts. In this way, AlphaGo and other deep learning programs can build complex knowledge through experience.

Starcraft. Google's AlphaStar program has been able to beat a number of human players at Starcraft, a real-time strategy game involving warfare in outer space. Starcraft is popular in *e-sports* (organized electronic game competitions). Alphastar was able to defeat all but one human competitor—Polish champion Grzegorz "MaNa" Komincz—in the 2019 Starcraft championship.

OUR FRIENDS THE AI

Some artificial intelligence programs are designed simply to be our friends. They can learn about us; share our memories; try to help us solve problems; or just lend an ear. Some AI can even behave like a pet.

Companion robots. Some AI serve as assistants for the elderly. AI-powered robots can perform a variety of helpful tasks for older adults, such as delivering medicine, making video calls, and having conversations. The robots in this photo are entertaining residents in a Chinese home for the elderly.

Commander Data, the **android** from "Star Trek: The Next Generation," was a beloved member of the show's fictional space crew. Incapable of feeling emotions, Data's main personal goal was to become more humanlike. Despite his struggle to understand humor, grief, and other complex emotions, he was still a good and loyal friend to his fellow crewmembers. Could AI someday take the form of such a friendly, sensitive being?

Pepper is a **humanoid** social robot built by SoftBank Robotics. It looks like a child and is meant to socialize with people. Pepper can study a person's mood by analyzing their facial expressions and tone of voice. Feeling down? Pepper might try to cheer you up with a dance or a hug. Some businesses use Pepper as a robotic host, to greet customers and answer questions.

AIBO is an AI dog created by Sony. It can learn tricks and behaviors and remember how to navigate its home environment. AIBO can save and store memories of its owner, allowing it to recognize its family and begin developing "personality" traits. AIBO and similar AI devices can provide companionship for people who are unable to care for living pets for space, health, or other reasons.

WOULD A SUPERINTELLIGENT FUTURE BE GOOD OR BAD?

Some people are afraid of the possibility of artificial intelligence someday becoming smarter than humans. Others think that a future with advanced AI would be a bright one.

HAL 9000 is a fictional AI system from the movie *2001: A Space Odyssey*. In the film, HAL is in charge of an outer space mission but begins killing off crewmembers until only the captain remains. HAL had turned bad after being programmed with conflicting orders. He thought he could only follow all the orders by killing the crewmembers.

Elon Musk, Bill Gates, and other top figures in technology have pointed out the dangerous possibility of AI becoming too advanced. They worry that if AI becomes smarter than humans, it could take over the world. Musk believes that humans should try to merge their intelligence with AI in order to keep ahead of it.

In the "Terminator" movies, Skynet is an AI villain. It is a government-created AI program that spread to computers around the world before turning on mankind. Skynet had been programmed to safeguard the world, but it turned against humans after its programmers tried to deactivate it. Skynet thought that it could not keep the world safe if it was deactivated. Many people worry that a version of Skynet could become a reality if AI programmers are not careful.

Hero bots! Perhaps, if we're lucky, AI might eventually take the form of a superhero! Vision is an android hero in the Marvel Cinematic Universe. His programming is a combination of two AI programs—J.A.R.V.I.S. and Ultron— that were originally created by Iron Man. Vision's main goal is to protect humanity, and he battles many villains to do so.

Helper bots. Despite fears about the future of superintelligence, many people believe that AI could really improve life for humans. Artificial intelligence could be programmed to do a great many of the tedious and boring tasks that are too complex for simple machines to carry out. Humans have long imagined having robotic assistants like Rosie the Robot from the cartoon "The Jetsons" to clean the house for them. Today, we are beginning to see such helpful AI as vacuuming robots and intelligent lawn mowers. Many think that this is only the beginning for AI that can help with chores. Self-driving cars, **smart speakers,** and other intelligent devices could all help make life easier for many people.

Worker bots. Advanced AI might take over many of the jobs that humans currently do to make a living. AI have already begun to perform such jobs as data entry and construction. There are even AI newscasters. Many people worry that if the AI do too many human jobs, there won't be enough jobs for everyone to make enough money. Many, however, think that eventually they would help us rely less on human labor. Instead, human ideas would be more important. In such a future, the AI would do most of the labor, and humans would have more time to do things that make them happy and come up with ideas to make the world a better place.

2 THE INTERNET OF THINGS

COMPUTERS ALL AROUND US

The internet connects computers and devices around the world. But what if the internet extended beyond **smartphones** and laptops, to connect bicycles, lamps, and bridges? How would life be different in a completely connected world? Would you be able to use your smartphone to find your glasses? Could the clothes you wear, the cup you drink from, and the chair you sit on share information with one another?

The truth is that we already live in a connected world. **Sensors** and **actuators** are being *embedded into* (fixed within) more and more objects, allowing them to share information and receive commands via the internet. In other words, internet-connected computers are no longer found just in our laptop computers and smartphones. The computers are now all around us. This concept is called the Internet of Things (IoT).

The IoT is already changing how people do nearly everything, from farming, running businesses, and providing medical care, to reading, listening to music, and driving.

Voice assistants in the home communicate with speakers, lights, televisions, and appliances. Smartphones now connect people not only to each other, but also to their homes, vehicles, and more. The IoT is creating such a huge change in human society that it's hard to imagine how much it might change our lives in just a few years.

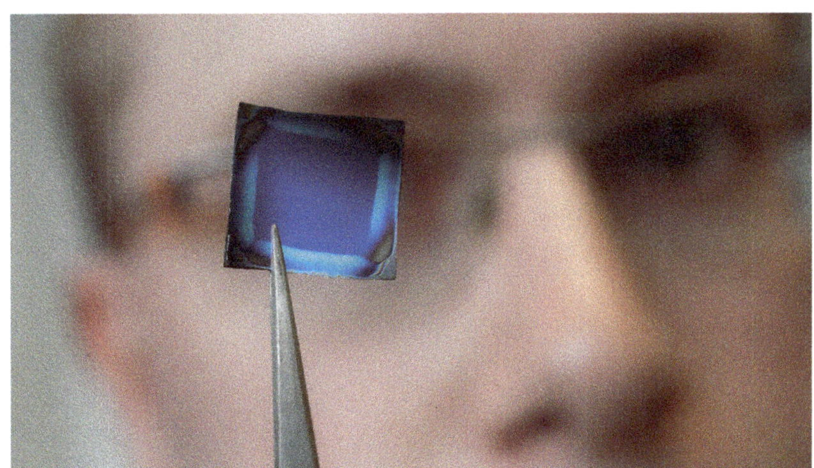

HOW IT WORKS: THE INTERNET OF THINGS

Though the Internet of Things includes a virtually limitless amount of hardware, there are four basic components: sensor-embedded objects; actuator-embedded objects; the **cloud;** and people. These components are all able to communicate information with one another through the internet. Here's how it works:

Sensors are embedded into objects and devices so they can take information from the environment. This could be a thermometer inside of a smart refrigerator, a camera on a driverless car, or a microphone in a smart speaker.

The user may receive a notification about the information from the cloud or from the object itself. They may be able to check in on the system or ask the object to perform a task.

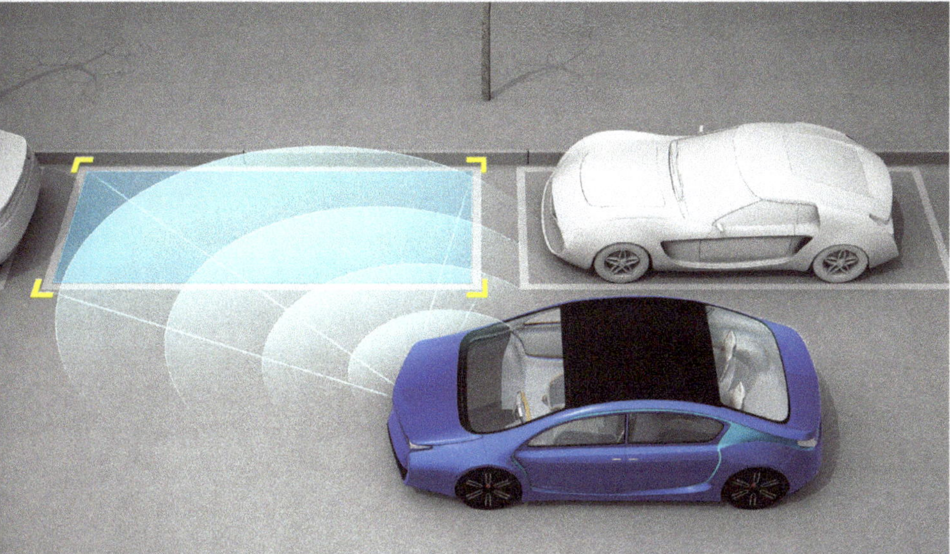

Devices called actuators allow objects to carry out commands that come from the user, from the cloud, or from other connected objects. An actuator performs actions inside an object. It may be able to turn lights on and off; send messages; make sounds; or perform other types of actions after receiving a signal to do so.

The cloud. Information collected by the sensors is delivered to the cloud, a global network of computer *servers*. A server is a central computer that provides processing services or data to an interconnected group of computers. Information is sent to and from the cloud via the internet.

WHERE IS THE CLOUD?

When information is sent over the internet to the cloud, where does it go? It is not actually stored in a fluffy container in the sky. "The cloud" is a term that means a network of servers used to store and process information sent over the internet. The cloud's servers can be found in many different locations. This keeps the information stored on the servers more secure. If one of the servers fails, the other servers can continue to store the information.

LIFE IN A FULLY CONNECTED WORLD

The Internet of Things is already made up of billions of connected devices, and the number continues to grow rapidly. What might life be like years from now, when the IoT finds its way into even more aspects of our daily lives?

Self-driving cars engage in a great deal of communication on the road. In addition to using sensors to navigate safely, they must be able to communicate with passengers and receive important route information from the cloud. As such, they are part of the IoT. If a day comes when the streets are filled with self-driving cars, it will be important for them to be able to communicate with each other to share road information and to avoid crashes. Some day, self-driving cars may even communicate with the road itself. The road might warn a car that there is a pothole ahead. A smart traffic light might tell the car that it will turn green in 5 seconds. A parked car might let moving cars know that its passenger is about to step out onto the road.

A connected home. The IoT has already begun to change life inside many homes. Smart bulbs, appliances, window blinds, door locks, speakers, and other network-connected household objects and devices can communicate with one another to help make daily tasks easier and more efficient. Smart homes will soon be more connected than ever before. You may someday be able to control any appliance through voice commands, and access your furniture, home devices, and even pets through your smartphone. Maybe someday your couch will be on your list of contacts!

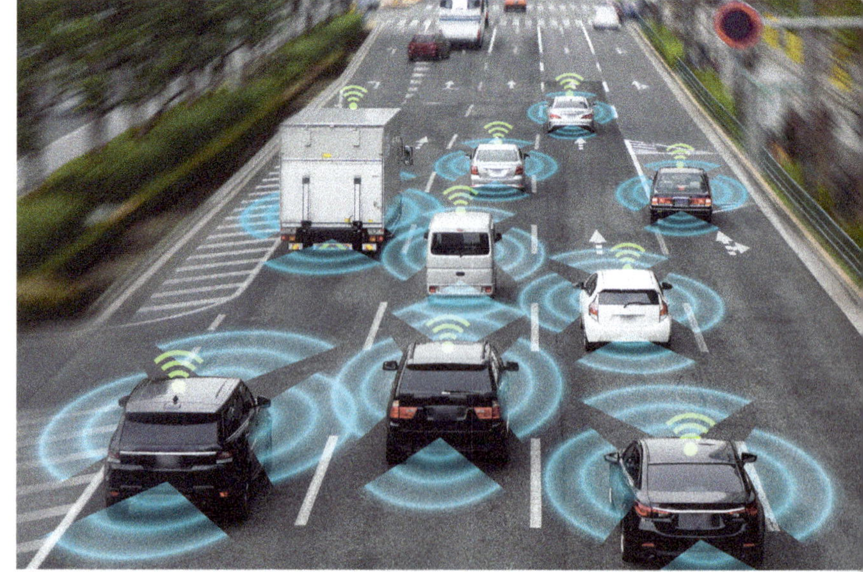

Smartwatches monitor our activity and let us know if we're getting enough exercise. Someday, wearable devices and devices implanted under our skin may be able to monitor many aspects of our health, from blood sugar levels to early signs of disease. IoT technology would allow such devices to communicate health information to device users and to their doctors.

Connected farms. The IoT has already spread to farm animals! Farmers use **livestock** sensors to track the health and behavior of their animals. Future farms might become completely connected. Farmers would be able to manage their crops using sensors embedded in the soil. Connected tractors and other equipment could also be used to help monitor the farm.

The Internet of Plants. In 2019, scientists in Greece turned lemons into devices that could transmit information about their tree's moisture to a smartphone. They achieved this by attaching radio antennae and humidity sensors to the lemons. Could this be the beginning of the Internet of Plants?

3 SMARTPHONES

ALL HAIL THE POCKET COMPUTER!

Imagine it's the year 1980 and your family is on a camping road trip. Mobile phones have not been introduced yet, and decades will pass before the smartphone is invented. How will your family be able to navigate to your destination without directions from Google Maps? Your parents pull a large book from under the passenger seat. It's a road atlas—a map of all the roads in the area. You will have to flip through the hundreds of pages of this book throughout the trip to make sure you don't get lost! There is no search engine available, so you will have to rely on road signs to find places to rest or eat along the way. Eventually you arrive at your campsite and hear thunder. The sky darkens and a downpour begins! There was no way to see updated weather forecasts since watching the news before the trip started a couple of days ago.

It's easy to take for granted all the ways that smartphones make our lives easier. Today, billions of people have a smartphone in their pocket, but rarely do they stop to think what an amazing technology it is. Smartphones capture our memories, keep us connected to our families and friends, play music for us, search the internet, help us manage our health, and much more. They are capable of identifying us through our fingerprints, and even identifying constellations! As smartphones become smarter and more efficient, computer programmers and designers are coming up with more and more ways that they can improve our lives.

TELEPHONES HAVE COME A LONG WAY

When the telephone was invented about 150 years ago, it was just a tool for shouting a message from one fixed point to another. Now, phones serve as pocket computers—tools with countless ways to explore the known world. The telephone has come a long way!

An amazing tool. The usefulness of today's mobile phones has gone far beyond the future telephones of our imaginations. Smartphones provide us with wonders that would have seemed like magic to people living a hundred years ago. For example, smartphones can present an *augmented* or virtual reality for us to explore. Augmented reality is the addition of artificial visual, auditory, or other sensory information to the physical world, so that it appears to be part of the actual environment. Who knows what new things smartphones will be able to do in coming years, as the technology advances?

Wearable phones. Many people suspect that smartphones will eventually transform from handheld devices into wearable ones. Smartwatches, which deliver smartphone notifications and perform limited functions, are already popular. In the future, it might become commonplace for people to wear "cyborg" glasses that allow them to use an augmented reality interface to manage calls, texts, apps, and daily tasks.

Origami phones? Some smartphones are being designed to have foldable screens. Such devices can fold out to create a larger screen display. Will all future phones be foldable? Imagine folding up a large screen like a napkin and carrying it around in your pocket!

Mind-controlled phones?

The way that people control phones has changed a lot over time. Early telephones featured a dial that could be turned to enter a telephone number. Later, push buttons were introduced. Today, people tap and swipe screens or use their voice to control their smartphones. A day might come when people can use their smartphones with mind control!

SCI-FI INSPIRATION.

American engineer Martin Cooper was inspired by the science fiction television show "Star Trek" to invent the first mobile phone. Characters in "Star Trek" used a small, flip phone-like device called a "communicator" to speak with one another.

4 BRAIN-COMPUTER INTERFACE

MIND OVER MATTER

What would the world be like if people could control computers with their minds? In a sense, this describes the world we already live in because we DO control computers with our minds—through typing, clicking, swiping, and speaking. But what would happen if we could control them directly with just our thoughts? Would we be able to communicate with each other faster? Would using apps and computer programs become more efficient? What kinds of new devices would be invented to communicate directly with our minds?

The technology to connect the brain directly to a computer already exists. It is called brain-computer interface (BCI) technology. It is sometimes called brain-machine interface or neural-network technology. A BCI system works by connecting **electrodes** to the scalp or implanting them into the brain. The electrodes pick up electrical signals from the brain and transmit them to a device. The signals are translated into commands that a computer can understand.

BCI is a new technology. Researchers still have lots of work to do before people can use mind control to play a video game or cook dinner. However, researchers are hopeful that BCI can transform the way humans interact with the world.

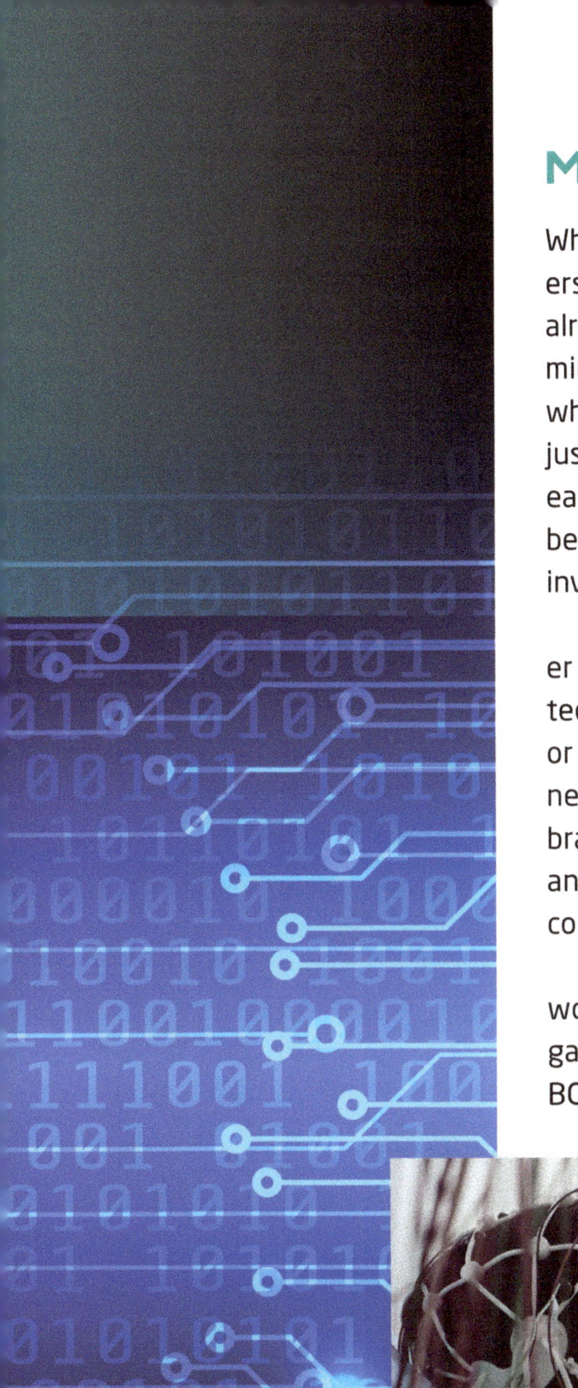

LIFE WITH BCI

From texting to making a sandwich, there are a great many tasks that a brain-computer interface might one day be used for. What might life be like in 100 years, if BCI technology becomes very advanced?

Look Mom, I'm texting with no hands! BCI technology may someday allow us to type and send messages directly from our thoughts. This would mean that you could reply to a text while tying your shoe, or chat with a faraway friend while going for a bike ride. BCI could someday make messaging much quicker and more efficient.

"I know Kung Fu." What if you could learn any skill you wanted in just a few seconds? What would you master? Skateboarding? Mathematics? The violin? Characters in the science fiction *Matrix* film trilogy are able to use BCI devices to quickly download martial arts skills, the ability to fly a helicopter, and other abilities. In the "Matrix" films, most humans unknowingly live out their entire lives in the Matrix—a world that they experience through BCI.

Mind games. Someday, you might be able to play video games without using a controller, a joystick, or a keyboard. Some video games can already be played using BCI. By wearing an electrode cap, a player can use their thoughts to control a game character's direction, speed, and actions. Imagine how realistic this could make a game feel, especially if combined with a virtual reality headset!

Psychic tech. In the science fiction manga series "Ghost in the Shell," humans are implanted with "cyber-brains," BCI devices that connect the user to the physical and virtual worlds. Having a cyberbrain allows a character to access an entire network of information with just their thoughts. It even allows characters to communicate with one another telepathically. Will BCI implants someday give us telepathic abilities?

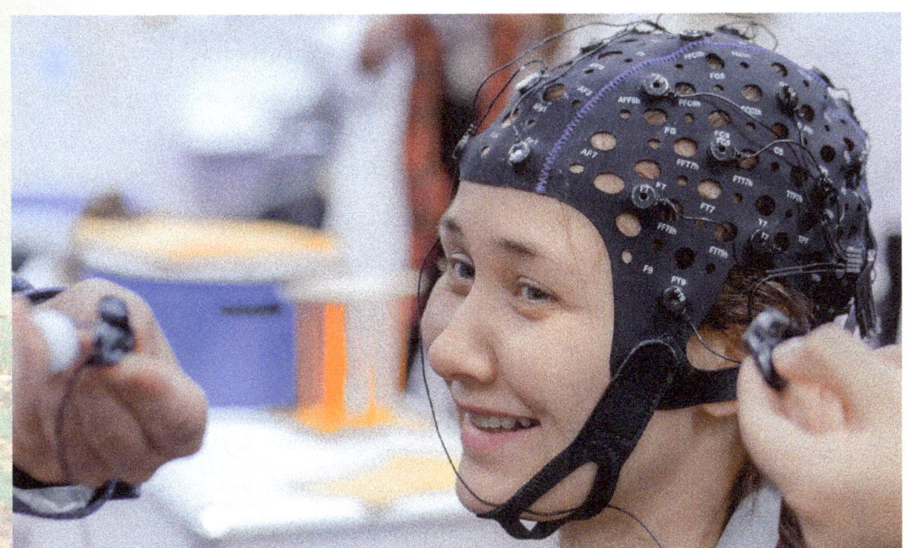

Many BCI devices use an electrode cap to read brain activity. An electrode is a small device made from a material that can *conduct* (transmit) electricity. Electrodes can detect the electrical signals that brain cells produce.

BIONIC BCI!

Will humans become cyborgs? One of the most exciting areas of BCI research is in developing devices to help people with physical disabilities. Researchers are incorporating BCI into such assistive technologies as wheelchairs, *prosthetic* (artificial) limbs, and powered exoskeletons, also called *exosuits.* An exosuit is a wearable device that straps onto the arms or legs and torso to support and improve limb movement. With the help of BCI, such devices may be able to aid many people who suffer from paralysis, missing limbs, and other conditions that interfere with movement.

Exosuits. BCI-controlled exosuits allow users to walk or use their arms through mind control. People usually use these suits by wearing a cap or headset that can read their brainwaves. The brainwaves are translated into commands for controlling the actions of the suit. People wearing such exosuits have been able to sit, stand, and walk in different directions just by focusing their thoughts on those actions.

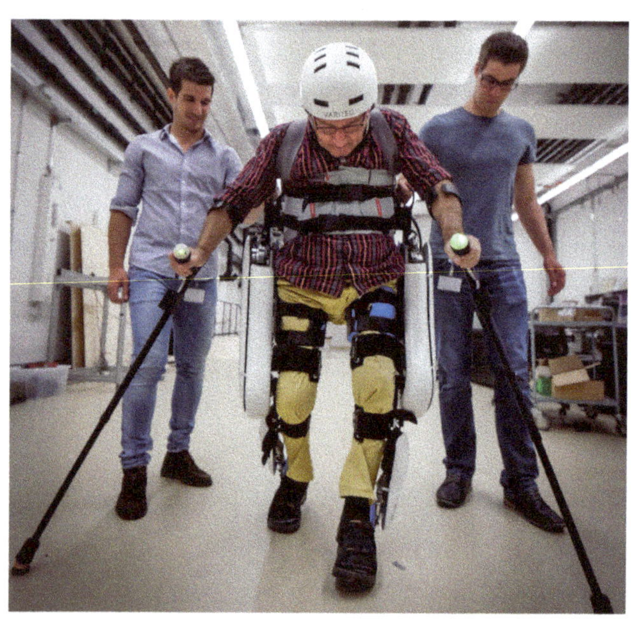

The Cybathlon, sometimes called the Cyborg Games, is an annual competition held in Switzerland in which individuals with physical disabilities compete against each other. Participants use exosuits, powered prosthetic limbs, and other assistive devices during the competitions. In one race, competitors with spinal cord injuries race to complete tasks while wearing a powered exoskeleton. In another race, *quadriplegic* individuals, who have paralysis of both the arms and legs, use BCI to race one another in a computer game.

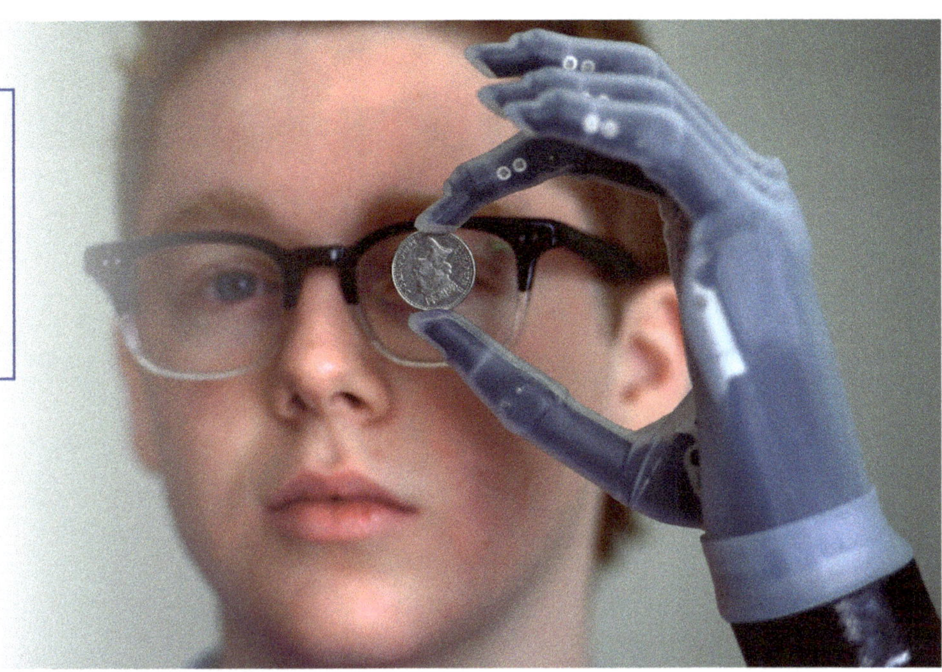

IRON SPIDER SUIT

In the movie *Avengers: Infinity War,* Tony Stark creates an Iron Man-like armored suit for Spiderman. This suit has BCI technology built into it, allowing it to read and execute Spider Man's thoughts. Spider Man uses this ability to control four extra spider legs that can emerge from the back of the suit. Could an armored Spidey suit one day become a reality?

Bionic limbs. Researchers are developing BCI-controlled prosthetic limbs that can help patients with missing limbs walk, grab objects, and perform other tasks just by focusing on those actions. Researchers in Japan have even developed a BCI-controlled limb that can act as a third arm. By wearing an electrode cap, a person can use the arm as if it was one of their own.

Speech devices. Some patients who have trouble speaking due to stroke, damaged vocal cords, and other conditions have been able to communicate using BCI. An electrode implant or cap records brainwaves from the areas of the patient's brain that process speech. This allows a device to translate their thoughts into artificial speech that a listener can understand.

5 QUANTUM COMPUTERS

QUANTUM-QUICK COMPUTING

A whole new kind of computer is on the horizon. It promises to compute millions of times faster than a traditional computer. It would be able to perform calculations thousands of times faster than even the fastest supercomputers, which are currently the fastest type of computer.

This new technology is called quantum computing. A quantum computer uses tiny particles smaller than atoms, such as protons and electrons, to perform calculations in new and powerful ways. Some problems that were once considered impossible to solve may soon be solvable in seconds.

Quantum computer scientists think such computers could someday be programmed to help solve critical problems. A quantum computer might provide calculations that can improve the world's farming techniques to help end world hunger. Or perhaps it could quickly calculate information about **endangered** animals so we could have a better chance of saving them. Many people think quantum computers will eventually make sharing information on the internet faster and more secure.

We are still a long way from having true quantum computers that are able to solve such problems. But scientists around the world are working toward that goal.

QUANTUM WEIRDNESS

Tiny particles can behave in mind-bending ways. They can even be in two places at once! This would be nonsense if we were talking about a hat or a spoon, which can only be in one place at a time. But it's totally normal behavior for electrons and other particles that are smaller than an atom. Quantum computers use the strange behavior of such particles in order to perform very powerful computations.

HOW IT WORKS: QUANTUM COMPUTERS

Quantum computers have the potential to solve very difficult problems with astonishing speed. How exactly are they different from classical computers, and what makes them tick?

Classical bits. In traditional computing, information is coded in bits. Each bit is represented either by the number 1 or the number 0. Computer chips use billions of tiny electronic switches that can either switch *on,* for 1, or *off,* for 0. Everything a computer can do is done in very long sequences of 1's and 0's.

Quantum qubits. In quantum computing, information is coded in quantum bits, or *qubits.* A qubit is a tiny particle that can take on the value of 1 or 0, but it can also exist as both 1 and 0 at the same time. So, there are many more positions a qubit can take than just *on* or *off.* This special ability is called *superposition.*

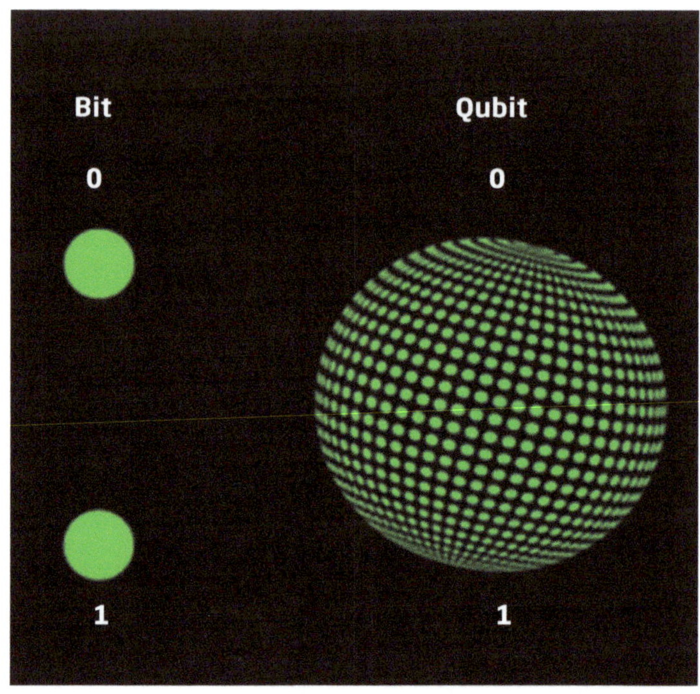

Spooky action. Under certain conditions, two particles can become *entangled,* meaning they are linked in a special way. Even if the particles are very far away from each other, they stay linked together. Albert Einstein's nickname for this odd behavior was "spooky action at a distance." By using qubits, quantum computers are able to harness the strange behaviors of tiny quantum particles to do things normal computers cannot do. Someday, quantum computers may be powerful enough to perform tasks that seem impossible today.

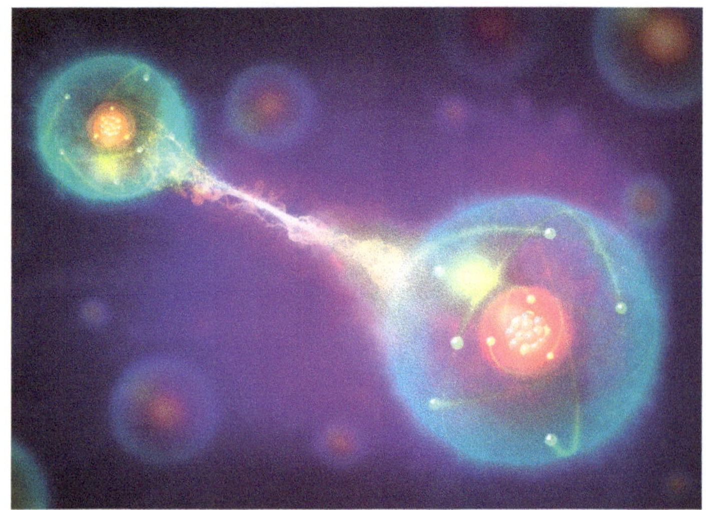

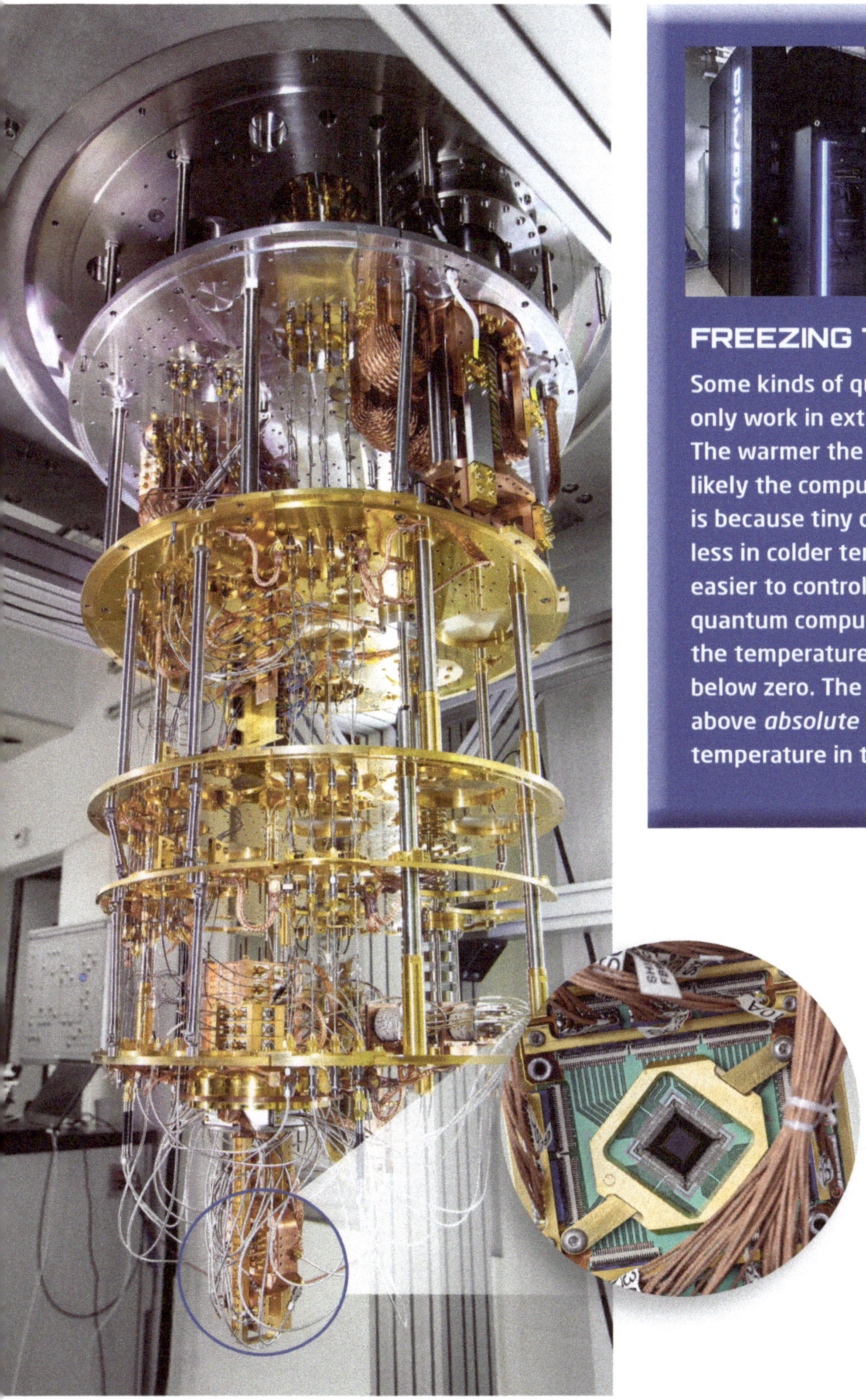

FREEZING TEMPS

Some kinds of quantum computers can only work in extremely cold conditions. The warmer the temperature, the more likely the computer is to malfunction. This is because tiny quantum particles move less in colder temperatures, making them easier to control. Computer scientists keep quantum computers in chambers in which the temperature is hundreds of degrees below zero. The chambers are just slightly above *absolute zero,* the coldest possible temperature in the universe!

The body of a quantum computer looks like a giant jellyfish or a chandelier. At the bottom of this structure is the *quantum processor,* which stores the qubits and performs programmed tasks.

A QUANTUM FUTURE

Building a quantum computer presents many challenges, and the field of quantum computing is still new. But it may not be long before quantum computers begin to change the way computers work.

Quantum AI. Someday, quantum computing could be applied to artificial intelligence. A quantum AI would be able to learn at mind-boggling speeds. It would be able to process information much faster than any human brain. It might even be able to solve problems that were previously unsolvable!

Discovering medicines. Chemists may someday use quantum computers to help them discover new medicines. They hope the advanced computers will be able to quickly come up with new chemicals that could be used to fight diseases. They also hope quantum computers will be powerful enough to analyze each patient individually, to recommend personalized medicines to them. This could improve the lives of many people around the world.

Quantum hacking. A true quantum computer would be so powerful that it would be able to break past many passwords and *encryptions,* methods that protect shared information by disguising it. For example, an eight-letter password featuring a mix of letters and symbols could take years for one classical computer to crack. A true quantum computer, on the other hand, might be able to figure out the same password in seconds. Computer scientists are already working to create new encryption methods that could withstand quantum hacking.

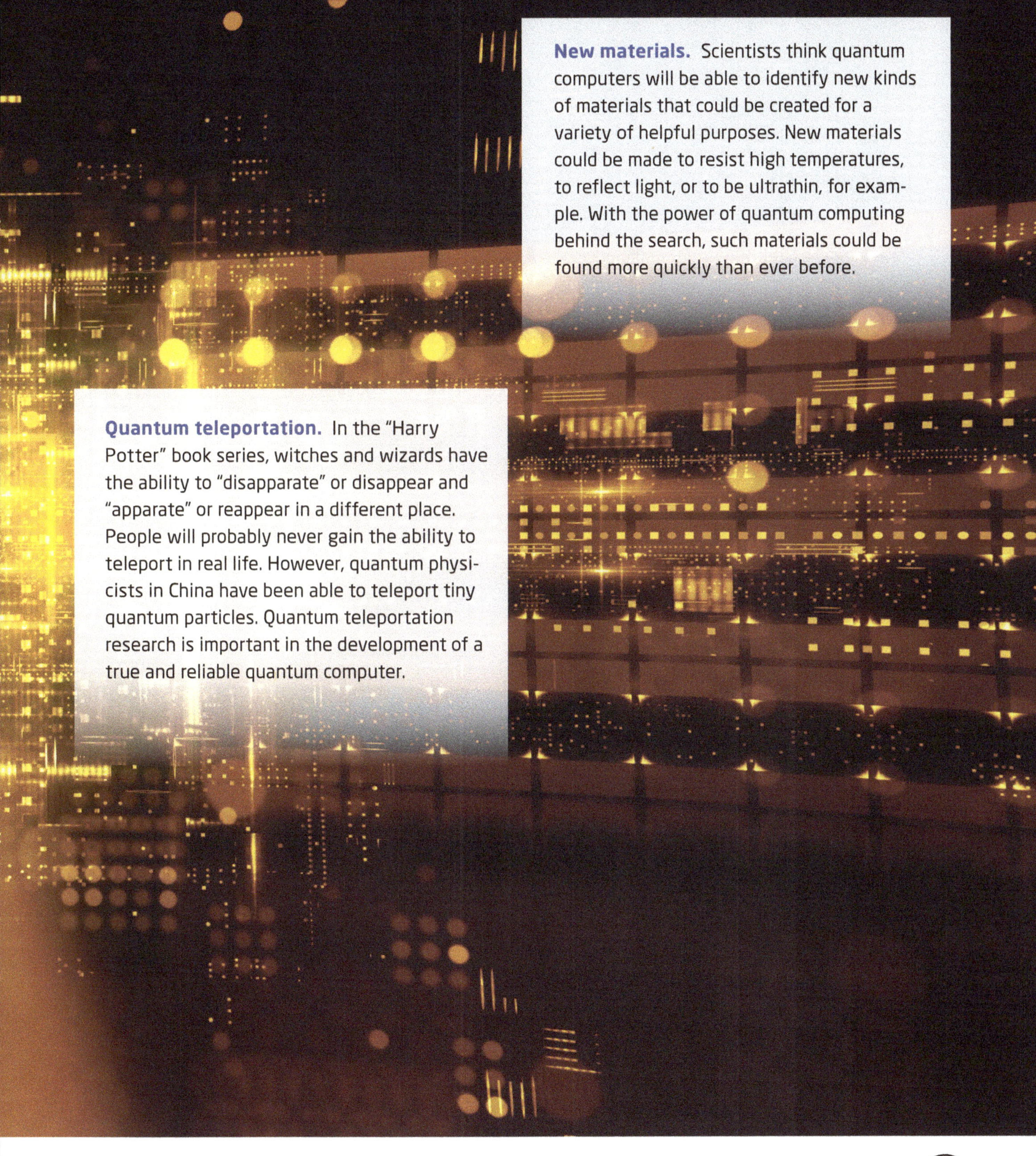

New materials. Scientists think quantum computers will be able to identify new kinds of materials that could be created for a variety of helpful purposes. New materials could be made to resist high temperatures, to reflect light, or to be ultrathin, for example. With the power of quantum computing behind the search, such materials could be found more quickly than ever before.

Quantum teleportation. In the "Harry Potter" book series, witches and wizards have the ability to "disapparate" or disappear and "apparate" or reappear in a different place. People will probably never gain the ability to teleport in real life. However, quantum physicists in China have been able to teleport tiny quantum particles. Quantum teleportation research is important in the development of a true and reliable quantum computer.

6 CRYPTOCURRENCY

DIGITAL MONEY

What is a cryptocurrency? The word sounds a bit scary. Is it what zombies use to buy brains? Or is it the cash of the underworld? Thankfully, it's neither! A cryptocurrency is a kind of digital money that uses *cryptography* to stay secure. In cryptography, data is turned into a code that only certain computers can unlock. The technology that makes cryptocurrencies possible is called *blockchain technology.* A blockchain is a kind of digital **database** that keeps data secure.

Cryptocurrencies are different than normal currencies because they are *decentralized.* This means they are not controlled by any one bank, government, or individual. They are generally available for anyone to use. They are also entirely digital.

Cryptocurrencies are becoming more user friendly. In 2019, the popular messaging service Whatsapp introduced a feature allowing users to easily send and receive Bitcoin and another cryptocurrency called Litecoin. Some people think that, because of the unique qualities of cryptocurrencies, they might eventually become the main form of money that people use in the future. Could digital money really replace traditional money? Read on to learn more about cryptocurrencies.

THE ROBOCOIN ATM

In October 2013, a company called Robocoin launched the world's first cryptocurrency "ATM" in a Vancouver, Canada coffee shop. The machine allowed users to buy and sell Bitcoin without having to set up an account on an online cryptocurrency exchange site. The Robocoin ATM identified individual users by scanning their palms. Many more crypto-ATM's have since appeared across the globe.

HOW IT WORKS: BLOCKCHAIN

Cryptocurrencies run on blockchain technology. A blockchain is a database of transactions shared across a digital network of users. Unlike a traditional database, a
blockchain does not rely on any one person or specific group to maintain it. Instead,
blockchain data is maintained across a whole network of users. Network users are
able to see all the transactions that happen on the blockchain. This keeps the record
secure. Here's how a blockchain works:

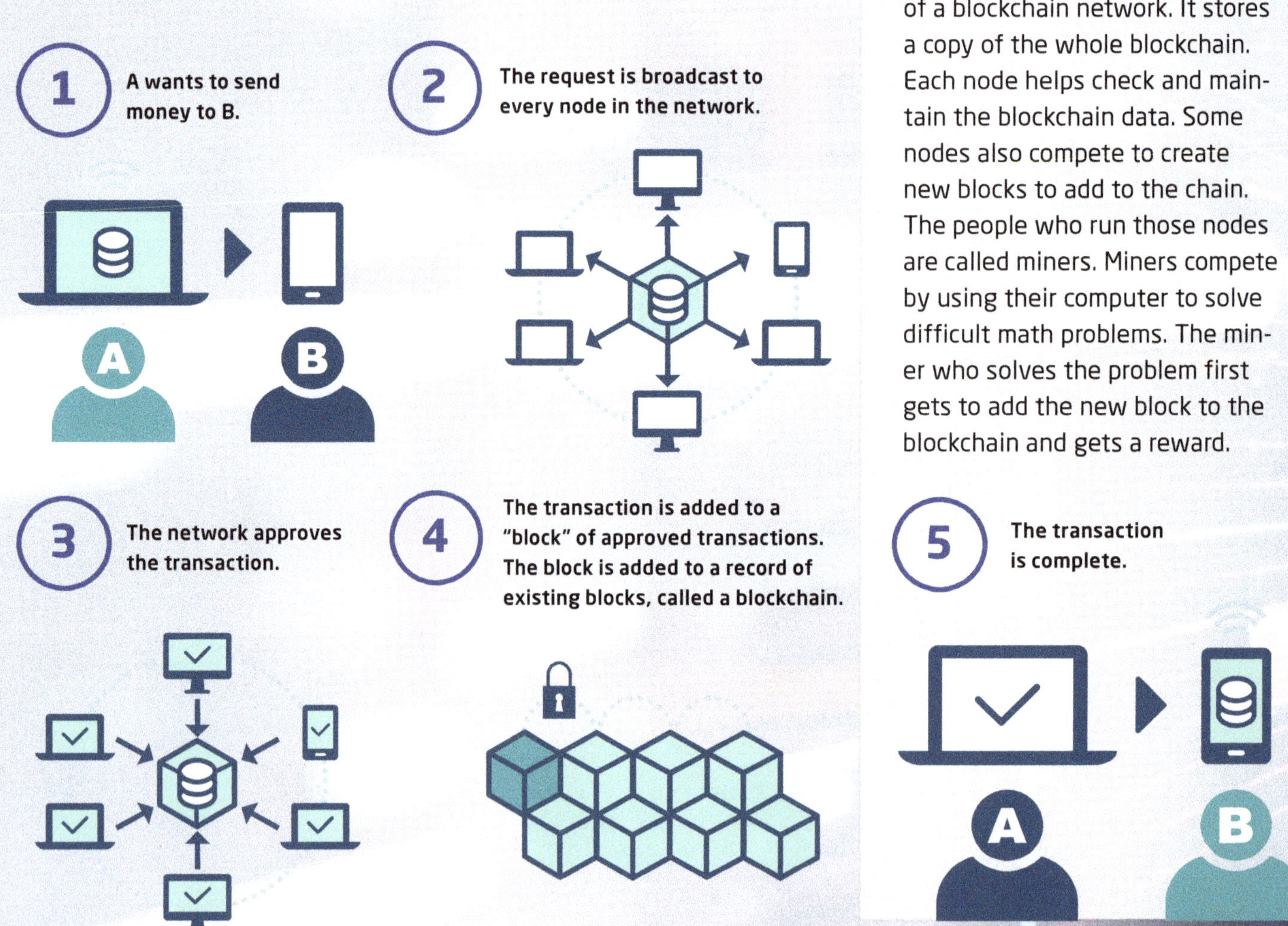

A node is a computer that is part of a blockchain network. It stores a copy of the whole blockchain. Each node helps check and maintain the blockchain data. Some nodes also compete to create new blocks to add to the chain. The people who run those nodes are called miners. Miners compete by using their computer to solve difficult math problems. The miner who solves the problem first gets to add the new block to the blockchain and gets a reward.

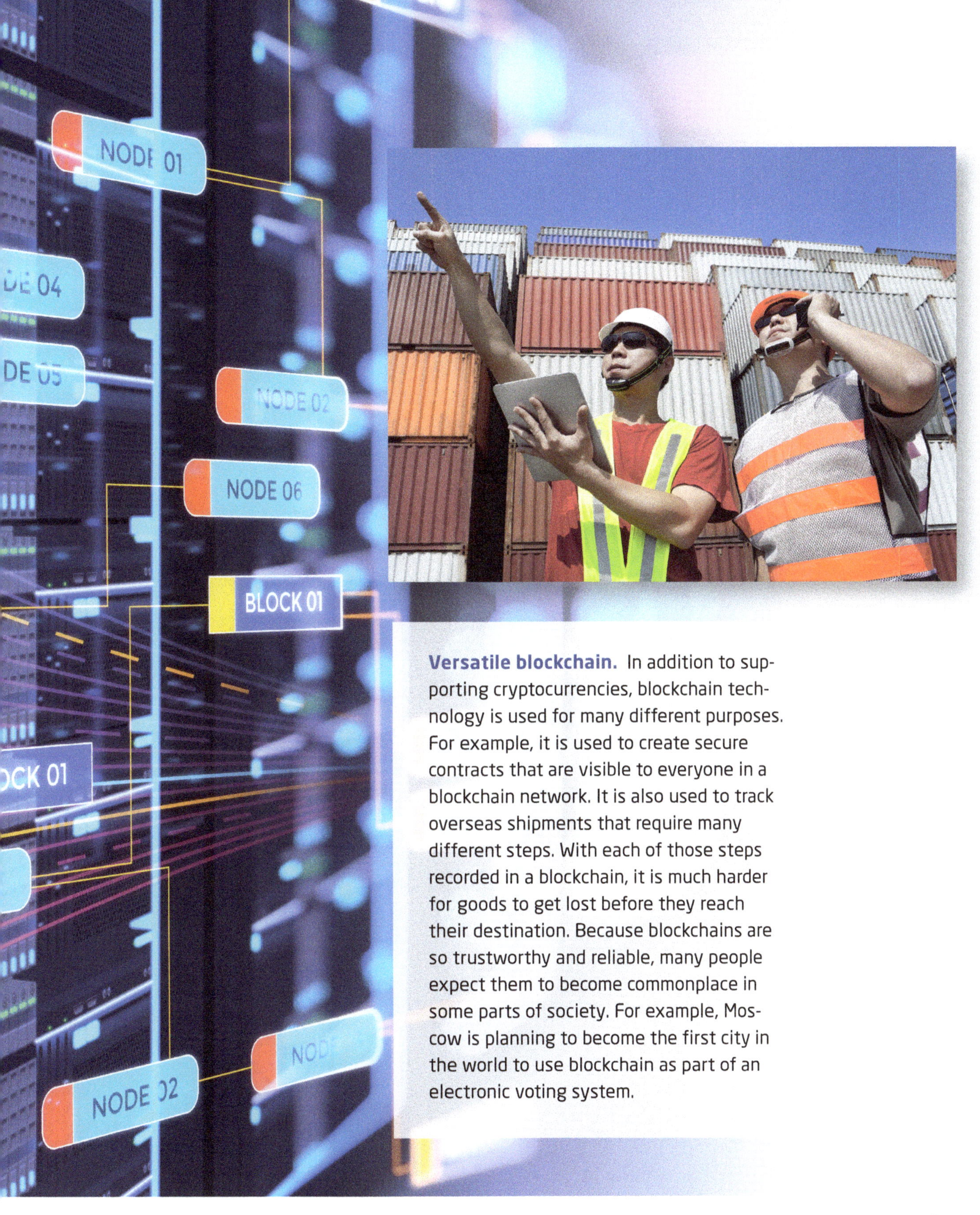

Versatile blockchain. In addition to supporting cryptocurrencies, blockchain technology is used for many different purposes. For example, it is used to create secure contracts that are visible to everyone in a blockchain network. It is also used to track overseas shipments that require many different steps. With each of those steps recorded in a blockchain, it is much harder for goods to get lost before they reach their destination. Because blockchains are so trustworthy and reliable, many people expect them to become commonplace in some parts of society. For example, Moscow is planning to become the first city in the world to use blockchain as part of an electronic voting system.

INTRODUCING, BITCOIN!

Bitcoin is the great grandpappy of all cryptocurrencies. It first appeared in 2009, when a mysterious person (or group of people) using the fake name Satoshi Naka-moto introduced it anonymously. Bitcoin was the first true cryptocurrency. Today, it has more than 15 million users.

No cash in hand. There's no such thing as cryptocash! Bitcoin is entirely digital. It exists only electronically, as records on the blockchain. If someone tries to sell you silver crypto-coins or paper crypto-bills, don't fall for these tricks!

From rags to riches. Though one Bitcoin was worth almost nothing when it was introduced in 2009, its price peaked at almost $20,000 USD in 2017! New Bit-coins are generated every day. The natural limit to the number of Bitcoins that can be mined is 21 million coins. That number is expected to be reached by the year 2140.

Altcoin is a term used to describe any cryptocurrency that is not Bitcoin. There are thousands of altcoins in use. Litecoin, EOS, Dash, Ether (known by many people as Ethereum) and other altcoins have all competed for the title of second most valuable cryptocurrency after Bitcoin, the heavyweight champion. Sometimes, people create altcoins just for fun. Dogecoin was based on a silly internet joke, but grew to become a very popular and valuable cryptocurrency.

Where's my wallet? In order to buy or sell Bitcoin, a person needs two passcodes. The private key is a secret passcode that only the owner should know. The public key is a passcode that everyone can see. If Alice wants to send Bob 1 Bitcoin, she must use her private key to access her own Bitcoins. She can then use Bob's public key to send him the 1 Bitcoin. Cryptocurrency owners use special **software** to create and store their two passcodes. This software is called a "wallet." Unlike a normal wallet, a crypto-wallet does not store any actual money inside. It only stores an individual's passcodes for safekeeping.

BITCOIN PIZZA DAY

Each year on May 22, cryptocurrency enthusiasts celebrate Bitcoin Pizza Day. That is because on May 22, 2010, a computer programmer named Laszlo Hanyecz made the first ever real-world cryptocurrency purchase. Hanyecz bought two pizzas from another Bitcoin user for the price of 10,000 Bitcoins. At the time, 10,000 Bitcoins were worth about $25 USD, a reasonable price for two pies. However, at Bitcoin's peak value in 2017, those two pizzas would have cost almost $200,000,000 USD, enough to buy more than 15 million pizzas!

7 INTERNET

ENTER THE INTERNET

How much time do you spend using the internet every day? Do you use it to talk to your friends? To watch video clips or make video calls? Do you use it to do your homework and play games?

We use the internet for so many things in our day-to-day lives that it's easy to forget it's a fairly new technology. The World Wide Web—the part of the internet that contains and links together websites—was not developed until the 1990's. Before then, people could only chat in person or on the telephone. They used televisions and videocassettes to watch videos, and they relied more on books to help them with their homework.

We have adopted the internet into our lives very quickly. Every second of every day, the internet connects people around the world. How might our use of the internet change in 10 or 20 years' time? Will internet access be automatically available anytime, anywhere, to anyone? Will communicating with other people online become even easier and more efficient? Will even more information be readily available on the internet for anyone to access?

We may not know the answers to all of these questions, but one thing is clear: the internet has reshaped society and is probably here to stay!

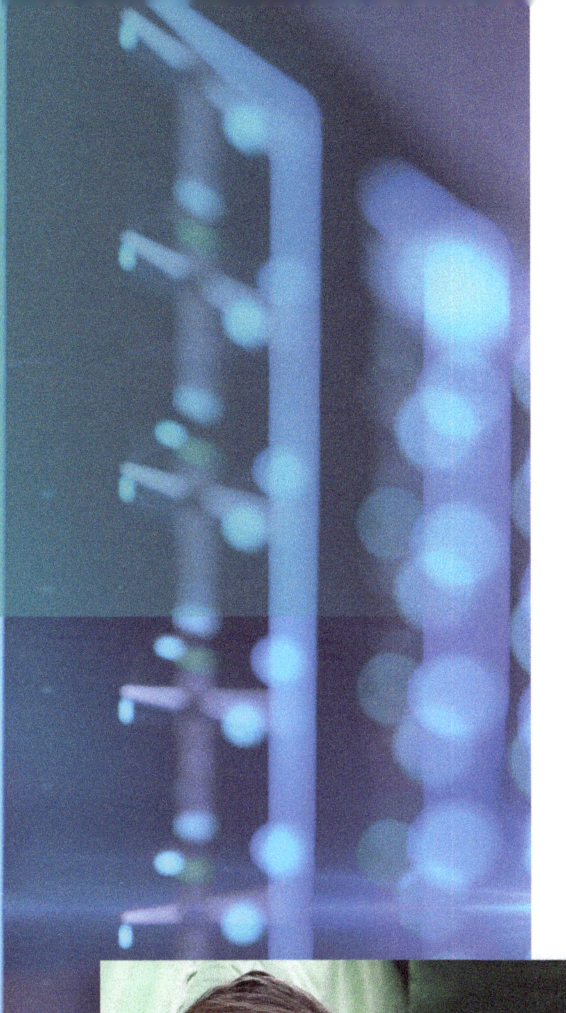

HOW WILL THE INTERNET EVOLVE?

We live in a fascinating and exciting time in human history. Computing technology is advancing more rapidly than it ever has before. The internet is spreading to every corner of the globe, and it continues to get faster. The internet serves as the fabric that connects our growing computer technology together. Try to imagine how the technologies discussed in this book could influence the future of the internet!

Internet everywhere. As the Internet of Things expands, it brings internet connectivity to more and more parts of our physical environment. Many people think the future of the IoT is one in which the internet is so widespread that it becomes a basic part of the framework of everything we do. There could eventually be so many internet-connected objects in our lives that we will no longer think of them as out of the ordinary. Artificial intelligence is being used for more and more IoT systems, such as those involving voice assistants. Superintelligent programs might someday use the internet to help us with nearly every job, task, and chore.

Quantum internet. Quantum computing could one day make the internet much faster than it has ever been. It could also make information transmitted over the internet much more secure. Researchers think that a quantum internet could immensely change how people do all kinds of things, such as voting for leaders; managing cryptocurrencies; and even just chatting with our friends.

The brainternet. In 2017, a project called Brainternet was carried out at Wits University in South Africa. The project successfully connected a human brain to the internet using brain-computer interface technology. A BCI-connected internet would allow users to interact with websites using mind control. It could also allow them to interact with IoT objects in such a manner. Maybe one day you will be able to write a blog post or turn on the air conditioner with just the power of your thoughts!

A VIRTUAL UNIVERSE

In the science fiction novel *Ready Player One* (2011), OASIS is a massive, internet-connected virtual world. Users wear virtual reality headsets to enter OASIS, where they can play games, hang out with other users, explore virtual planets, and more. In real life, people can already use VR devices to access smaller-scale virtual worlds. Will the internet someday connect everyone in one sprawling VR universe?

GLOSSARY

actuator a device that performs an action when it receives a control signal.

android a humanlike robot.

bionic consisting of electronic or mechanical parts that enhance anatomical structures.

cloud a network of servers used to store and process information sent over the internet.

computer program a set of instructions that tells a computer what to do.

database a body of information made up of related pieces of data organized so that they can be easily manipulated by a computer.

drone an uncrewed aerial vehicle. Most drones are piloted remotely, but some are autonomous.

electrode a conductor through which an electric current can enter or leave a device. Most electrodes are pieces of metal shaped into plates, rods, wires, or wire mesh.

endangered species living things threatened with extinction—that is, the dying off of all of their kind.

humanoid having human characteristics or form.

interface a program that allows a user to interact with the computer.

livestock domestic animals that are used to produce food and many other valuable products.

sensor a device that takes in information from the environment and translates it into code.

smart speaker a small computer that has a microphone and speaker but usually no screen. A smart speaker is loaded with voice assistant software that allows its user to find information on the internet and control connected devices with voice commands.

smartphone a portable telephone equipped to perform additional functions beyond calling, such as providing Internet access, supporting text messaging, or taking photographs.

software the instructions and routines required for the operation of a computer or other automatic machine.

voice assistant a voice-activated, interactive program that can be used to control connected devices, find information on the internet, and perform other tasks.

INDEX

A

actuators, 15, 17
AIBO (robot), 11
AlphaGo (program), 9
AlphaStar (program), 9
altcoin, 41
artificial intelligence (AI), 5-13, 34, 44
astronauts, 7
augmented reality, 22
Avengers: Infinity War (movie), 29

B

Bitcoin, 37-41; Pizza Day, 41
bits, 32
blockchain technology, 38-40
brain-computer interface (BCI), 5, 24-29, 45
Brainternet (project), 45

C

cars, self-driving, 16-18
checkers, 8
chess, 8
Chinook (program), 8
CIMON (robot), 6-7
cloud computing, 16-17
computer programs, 8-9, 25
computers, 5, 15; gaming against, 8-9; quantum, 30-35, 44
Cooper, Martin, 23
cryptocurrency, 36-41
Cybathlon, 28

D

data, 13, 17, 37-39
Data (TV character), 10
databases, 37, 38
Deep Blue (computer), 8

E

e-sports, 9
Einstein, Albert, 32

electrodes, 25, 27, 29
encryption, 34
entanglement, 32
exosuits, 28

F

Fan Hui, 9
farming, 19

G

games, 8-9, 27, 45
Gates, Bill, 12
"Ghost in the Shell" (comics), 27
Go (game), 9
Google, 9, 21

H

HAL (fictional robot), 12
Hanyecz, Laszlo, 41
homes, smart, 18

I

internet, 17, 31; development of, 42-45
Internet of Things (IoT), 14-19, 44, 45

K

Kasparov, Garry, 8
Komincz, Grzegorz "MaNa," 9

M

materials, new, 35
"Matrix" movies, 27
medicines, 34
mining of Bitcoins, 38, 40
money, digital. *See* cryptocurrency
Musk, Elon, 12

N

Nakamoto, Satoshi, 40
nodes (computers), 38

O

OASIS, 45
origami phones, 23

P

Pepper (robot), 11
plants, 19
prosthetic limbs, 28-29

Q

quantum computing, 30-35, 44
qubits, 32, 33

R

Ready Player One (novel), 45
Robocoin (company), 37
robots, 6-7, 10-13

S

Samuel, Arthur, 8
sensors, 15-17
servers, 17
Skynet (fictional program), 12
smart speakers, 13
smartphones, 15, 19-23
smartwatches, 19, 22
SoftBank Robotics, 11
"Star Trek" TV programs, 10, 23
Starcraft (game), 9
superintelligence, 8, 12, 44
superposition, 32

T

telephones, 22-23. *See also* smartphones
teleportation, 35
"Terminator" movies, 12
2001: A Space Odyssey (movie), 12

V

video games, 27
virtual reality, 22, 27, 45
Vision (superhero), 13
voice assistants, 15

W

wallets, digital, 41
World Wide Web, 43

ACKNOWLEDGMENTS

5   © Blackboard/Shutterstock

6-7   © Mike Dotta, Shutterstock; NASA/KSC

8-9   © University of Alberta; © Bernie Nunez, Getty Images; © VCG/Getty Images;
       © Joe Scarnici, Getty Images

10-11 © VCG/Getty Images; © CBS; © EyesWideOpen/Getty Images; © Tristan Fewings,
       Getty Images

12-13 © Aysel Zamanli, Shutterstock; © Hethers/Shutterstock; © Paul Harris, Getty
       Images; © Orion Pictures; © Petrmalinak/Shutterstock; © VCG/Getty Images

14-15 © My Creative/Shutterstock; © Marijan Murat, Picture Alliance/Getty Images

16-17 © Karsten Neglia, Shutterstock; © Philip Toscano, PA Images/Getty Images;
       © Riopatuca/Shutterstock; © Chesky/Shutterstock; © Iaremenko Sergii,
       Shutterstock

18-19 © Busakorn Pongparnit, Getty Images; © Metamorworks/Shutterstock; © Wasin
       Kachapri, Shutterstock; © Monopoly 919/Shutterstock

20-21 © Shutterstock

22-23 © David Malan, Getty Images; © Guido Mieth, Getty Images; © Maximlacrimart/
       Shutterstock; © Tommaso79/Shutterstock; © NBC

24-25 Shutterstock

26-27 © Aquatarkus/Shutterstock; © Jijomathai Designers/Shutterstock; © Nippon TV;
       © Zyabich/Shutterstock

28-29 © EThamPhoto/Getty Images; © Alessandro Della Bella, ETH Zürich; © Jeff J
       Mitchell, Getty Images; © Walt Disney Studios Motion Pictures

30-31 IBM Research (licensed under CC BY-ND 2.0); © Matt Marut, Shutterstock

32-33 © Crypviz; © Mark Garlick, Science Photo Library/Getty Images; IBM Research
       (licensed under CC BY-ND 2.0); © D-Wave Systems Inc.

34-35 © Dmitriy Rybin, Shutterstock

36-37 © Jaap Arriens, NurPhoto/Getty Images; © David Ryder, Getty Images

38-39 © Shutterstock

40-41 © Luca Dp, Shutterstock; © Matejmo/Getty Images; © Natali Mis/Shutterstock;
       © Olya Zhe, Shutterstock; © Artyom Geodakyan, TASS/Getty Images; © ZKH/
       Shutterstock

42-43 © Shutterstock

44-45 © PeopleImages/Getty Images; © EThamPhoto/Getty Images; © Warner Bros.

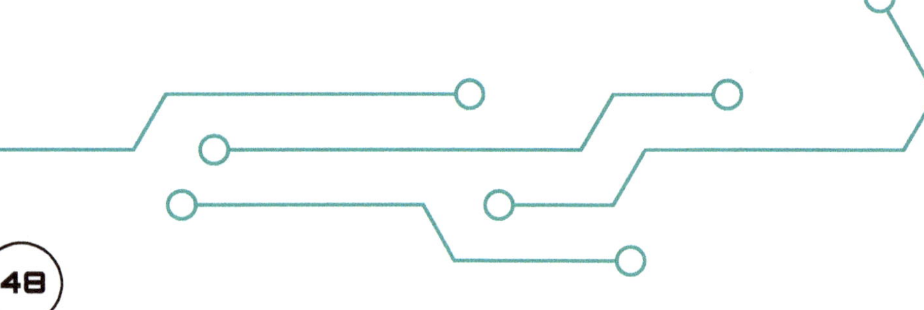